Red Beans and Ricely Yours

Winner of the 2005 T. S. Eliot Prize

The T. S. Eliot Prize for Poetry is an annual award sponsored by Truman State University Press for the best unpublished book-length collection of poetry in English, in honor of native Missourian T. S. Eliot's considerable intellectual and artistic legacy.

Judge for 2005: Ishmael Reed

Red Beans and Ricely Yours

poems by Mona Lisa Saloy

Truman State University Press
New Odyssey Series

Published by Truman State University Press, Kirksville, Missouri
tsup.truman.edu

Cover art: Leslie "Louisiana" Jones, *Strutting Their Stuff, a Second Line*.
1988, pen and ink and acrylic color. Used by permission of the artist.
Cover designer: Teresa Wheeler
Body type: Galliard, copyright Adobe Systems, ITCGalliard is a registered
trademark of International Typeface Corporation; display type: Optima,
copyright Linotype Library GmbH.
Printed by Thomson-Shore, Dexter, Michigan USA

Library of Congress Cataloging-in-Publication Data
Saloy, Mona Lisa.
  Red beans and ricely yours : poems / by Mona Lisa Saloy.
    p. cm. — (New odyssey series)
  ISBN 1-931112-53-3 (alk. paper) — ISBN 1-931112-54-1 (pbk. : alk.
paper)
  1. African Americans—Poetry. 2. New Orleans (La.)—Poetry. I. Title. II.
Series.
  PS3619.A439R43 2005
  811'.6—dc22

                                                          2005016917

For my family
and extended family

Contents

Black Creole Love

Red Beans and Ricely Black

Acknowledgments

Some poems in this collection were published in the following journals.

African American Review: "Word Works"

Black Scholar: "Marie Laveau" (earlier version of "The Ballad of Marie LaVeau")

Cricket: "French Market Morning," "For My Brothers"

Faulkner Society's Double Dealer: "Shotgun Life"

Ishmael Reed's Konch: "The N Word"

Louisiana Cultural Vistas: "French Market Morning," "Daddy Poem IV," "Recycling Neighborhood Style," "End Notes"

Lousiana English Journal: "On Writing," "A Few Words on My Words," "Daddy's Philosophy," "Jim Crow," "The Last Mile," "Summer in New Orleans, 1999," "Southern Sisters," "Heritage," "We've Come this Far," "End Notes"

Southern Review: "Song for Elder Sisters"

Some poems in this collection were published in the following anthologies.

Dark Waters, North West Anthology of Black Writers and Poets: "French Market Friend," "French Market Morning," "For Frank Fitch," "This Afternoon"

From a Bend in the River: 100 New Orleans Poets: "Word Works"

Furious Flower: African American Poetry from the Black Arts Movement to the Present: "The N Word," "For My Sister," "We've Come This Far"

Immortelles, Poems of Life and Death by New Southern Writers: "Charm Fails Death," "Villanelle for Voodoo"

This Far Together: Haight Ashbury Literary Journal 1980–1995: "For Frank Fitch," "For Nat King Cole Babies"

Word Up: Black Poetry of the 80s from the Deep South: "My Mother is the Daughter of a Slave...," "Frontliners"

Some poems in this collection appeared in the following newspapers.

Gambit Weekly: "This Afternoon"

San Francisco's Appeal to Reason: "For Frank Fitch"

Some poems appear in the following films.

Color: A Sampling of Contemporary African American Poetry (The Poetry Center and American Poetry Archives 1995): "For Frank Fitch"

Poets Sanctuary (New Orleans, 1998): "Crescent City Mambo" [here titled "Word Works"]

Word Works (Poets in the Dream State Video Anthology, New Orleans Film and Video Access Center, 2001): "Word Works"

"Hey there, Sugar Darlin', / Let me tell you something…" from "Groove Me," written by New Orleans-born R&B singer King Floyd (Malaco Productions, 1970).

Red Beans and Ricely Southern

Word Works

I'm about how words
work up a gumbo of culture,
stamped and certified African,
delivered on southern American soil.
In my word house,
we spit out articles and prepositions
like bitter chewing tobacco.
We lean on words that
paint pictures of *galait*
and grits and good times,
sittin' under gallery shades,
sippin' lemonade,
wearin' the afternoon
like a new dress.

This, my birthright,
gives a sense of place
that gets under your skin
like a swamp leech or a good story
out for blood.
The region gives you toast
or beignets with jam.
The R&B, blues, jazz, and reggae rhythms spice
Saturday-night suppers
and street parades,
when the Grand Marshall
leads the Second Line
after a funeral or
any good excuse to party
where umbrellas dance.

Folks all colored
from pale and yellow
to midnight blue-black
never just stand back and watch

they gon' say it how they see it
how they feel,
'bout everything and then some,
from roaches to do-rags,
from daddy-do-right
to David Ku Klux Duke,
to sisters wringing
the barest budget for another meal.

So, here's a taste,
begun in a roux,
sautéed in lines like
"Trust a man as far as you can see him,
cause you know,
stiff stuff don't have no conscience"
Sista Sarah said.

She had nine kids
and three grandkids,
didn't look a day over 40.
Said she was preserved because
"she left the fun box in and
took the trouble box out."
Then Hebert cut in from the curb,
and fun was all he heard.
Said he was
"the women's pet
the sissy's regret
and the whore's lollipop."
And Sista Sarah said well
"pass the bread, 'cause
that's baloney for true!"

So, call this a Crescent City mambo,
of days in peopled streets,

or nights in low-lighted clubs
on boulevards,
where passersby pale and bloom
like days-old irises or azaleas,
the places where neighborhood front porches
and side galleries stand vigil
for tall talkers
and pass-the-time rappers,
here, in my house,
a Crescent City mambo in words.

Back on the Block

Where shotguns sag in the middle,
like a yawn sometimes,
a porch tips
        or sinks into the ground like it
                swallowed more than rainwater.
Walk in the front door; see out the back door.
The banquette
        dips to nothing midblock
where sun-bleached white oyster shells line the street.

This is semitropics,
where green lizards squeeze through door jams.
Combat roaches march armies over dishes, pillows, and you after dark.
Spiders leave bump tracks over your face at sunup.
Fleas kiss and suck you sick.
Grapevines strangle windows and roof gutters.
Fire ants invade kitchen walls, sandals, and lingerie.
Louisiana is alive, and bees scream till dusk.
Then crickets cry till dawn
        and battle frogs for freedom.
Only the swamp swallows and coughs air,
        sneezes its mist into moonlight.

Where courtyards are the romantic meeting place
for doves and lovers,
between the louvered windows and french doors,
wooden dance floors dip
under tiled ceilings,
with potted begonias hanging
between palms and bricks.
I sweat,
        scratch heat bumps and 'squito bites.
Brown bugs bring my body to its knees.
Decay knows all seasons
        from steel blue-gray to bright pea green.

I sip mint tea,
           wipe my forehead with a hand towel,
                      fan myself to sleep.
The only strict lines are asphalt,
                       street lights, airport runways.
Even the banquette erupts under oak roots.

This Poem is for You My Sister

—for Barbara Ann

    Still eight years my elder
I remember clutching your circular felt skirt,
me, all snotty nosed and wanting your rhinestone sweater.
I remember wishing to follow you
to the zoo or the record shop
and being told to skip rope
or dream little Black-girl dreams
of saints, Voodoo queens, or guardian angels.
But you fed me Brooke Benton,
Dinah Washington, and Ella Fitzgerald as appetizers.
At 10, I was drunk on Nat King Cole,
Coltrane, and Miles Davis,
and my spirit would never be measured in years again.

    One fall, you ran from jim crow, left for Seattle,
our room full of your rose hip sachets,
your old green leather jacket,
and the straight skirts I had no hips to fill.
My life, shaken without you,
was empty like a finished Barq's root beer.
I wore loneliness like
your hand-me-down skirts.
When the record player screeched,
I heard your voice—hey girl—
between Johnny Mathis melodies:
        "When Sunni gets blue
        She breathes a sigh of sadness
        Like the wind that stirs the trees...."
Your face faint, floods me
with your Tchoupitoulas smile,
thick black braids,
never aging in your high school photo.

    After mother passed, and brother joined the Marines,
and Daddy drank his memories sour

and stale as day-old beer breath,
I wanted you to answer my anger,
to wipe my tears dry with a sock hop or
a backyard barbecue.

    So I followed your memory northwest, over Cascade
      mountains
and Suquamish tribes.
I heard mother's voice:
    "You mind good now ya hear.
    You mind your sister good, now."

    You, mother of a son,
wife to a man who believes love an unidentified emotion,
tenderness a foreign conspiracy.
Each season of mail a burden like horror,
the hell on his shoulders leaning on you like a sawhorse.

    Your hands are the color of gentleness and Pacific sand,
your breasts broken with years of curses cold as frostbite, and
our prayers melting each scream like fudge.
So sister love dipped in golden seal, mouthfuls of carrot juice and holy
    water,
broke the pain of those years like a finger snap or a joke.

    This poem is for you my sister
with your Tchoupitoulas smile,
your jet-black braids, that round bottom like mother's,
and your ankles that swell with the rain.

    Still eight years my senior,
time peels away.
Kiwi fruit memories stay with alfalfa seeds sprouting friendship
and globe-trotting; and as we skip across Caribbean beaches or Pacific
    shores,
we swim among warm crowds.

Your eyes soothe me
like the guardian angel of my childhood dreams.
We are masked in love
and mother's smile.

    This poem is for you my sister
with your Tchoupitoulas smile,
your jet-black braids,
that round bottom like mother's,
and your ankles that swell with the rain.

My Mother's the Daughter of a Slave

an early generation of free city-Black women,
New Orleans, 1907,
when jazz honked and tonked dives
in the Vieux Carré and uptown.
She was jet-black, and she was happy.
Never knew she was cute
'til a high yellow nigger named Louie came 'round.
Called Mother pretty black, almond eyes,
streetlight bright.
I never knew her grown.
She said, "live good *bébé*."

   She passed in '66,
knew everybody for blocks,
and they came every night for two weeks
to pay last respects.
Stood single file for two blocks on the banquette.
From sundown to starlight,
they came they said because they remembered.
Said she always had a wink, a smile,
and time to listen, or make big fun, or help, or be.
Always said, "live good every day;
it's all we've got."
And they came they said
because they remembered.

   She was jet-black, and she was happy.
Never knew she was cute
'til a high yellow nigger named Louie came 'round.
Called Mother pretty Black,
almond eyes, streetlight bright.
I never knew her grown. She said,
"live good *bébé*; it's all we've got."

For Frank Fitch

Papa was born a slave in Alabama
before the Civil War's end
or so he thought.
Said, the war'd been over since 1865,
and it must've been past '85
leaving the Fitch plantation for Mississippi then New Orleans.
Didn't nobody tell 'em that slavery was over,
was against the law to read and write,
but Papa figured it was time to be free.

Papa lived free with a youngun
he loved forever as his brother.
Neither one saw their momma.
Didn't need no proof, Artigis says,
When lanky Frank ate,
he ate too.
Papa said, "things get betta
and harda every day."
Said, "evva since their neck collars
(were) cut, they stuck
together like nappy hair on African folks
from the Fitch plantation
to New Orleans,"
to Papa's own Baptist Church,
Mt. Zion on North Robertson Street,
his too-many children, great-grandchildren,
and to television.
Past one hundred and ten,
Papa still called me a "yella child."
His tobacco wad of spit
landed just below the rim of his rusty tin
as he rocked on the front porch
smiling, thinking, and watching me
play in the dirt.

I watched Papa rock, and think, and smile every day.
Papa never got to see me sit freely
on busses or go to a white movie house.
Papa never knew I'd go to a white college or ride in an airplane.
Papa said, "things gonna be betta and harda
every day child."

Southern Sisters

There's a way
Crescent City women,
downtown brown sisters,
put a face towel
on their shoulders,
sweat rags for summers,
when it's hot enough
to melt toe cheese
on the banquette.

There's a way N'awlins women,
brick-head red sisters,
carry a kerchief
through long tan fingers;
it's like
the hand that fans you.

There's a way Crescent City sisters
throw a wink
with a wide smile.
So good,
makes you want to kiss yo' mamma, yeah,
makes you want to kiss yo' mamma, yeah.

There's a way the home
of hucklebuck women
tip a hat to the side on their heads
and strut—all dressed up to kiss—
like queens of the ebony isles.
makes you want to kiss yo' mamma, yeah,
makes you want to kiss yo' mamma, yeah.

Frontliners

We came after WWII
the doo-wop kids
the original teenagers
who believed in America
though second-class citizens
the last jim crow generation
often imitated from Jolsen to Elvis.
Our beat took the Chitterling Circuit to juke joints
        and nightclubs back of town.

    We made *Bandstand* and Motown
        anointed the world with soul and the Afro
        sewed freedom into America's vote
        and believed there was a place for us
        in the land of the free.

So, the youth moved north
bit the bitter freedom of blank faces
where everyone's from someplace else,
the taste of a modern era.

    Where's the Black community now?
In double-dutch contests
sponsored by McDonalds or
under the neon moon at the Grammys.

    I can count the Black men my age on one hand.
There's good brothers, married bloods,
died- or wish-they'd-died-in-Vietnam brothers,
street brothers, or die-now-in-prison ones.
Warriors left, the brothers now on the front lines
hold on to their blackness and sanity like a last meal.

    Where's the Black community now?
Burrowed warmly in our hearts,
rising in a melody or two, or a good gospel shout at Sunday service.

We live from Atlantic to Pacific,
send our love by stamp or phone call,
see our traditions on dance floors of clubs
where DJs scratch to "tenders" in Reeboks
or Jordache & Guess jackets.

Oh yeah. We still speak Black.
Ghettoese is now hip enough to get airplay
from radio to video,
and the times are tighter than a turtle's tale.
The government won't give a crippled crab a crutch.

So we smell of sweat and the sobbing of lean years.
We know how to cry and hold each other
no matter how many statistics publish lies about how
we don't or can't stay married.
We've looked north long enough.
Saw promises fade with each dusk.
We grew inside America like oak trees and Louisiana pine.
The eagle still pays up.
We pinch the nickels in our pockets 'til the buffalo squeals,
and thank God for weekends.

We grow lean,
dig soul on the commute to work,
whisper on sidewalks, and celebrate minutes.
Our children skip to ghetto blasters, MP3 players.
We escaped America's change like chameleons.
We know how to live
jusqu'aux bontemps rouler—
until the good times roll.

Louisiana Log

—for Bob Kaufman

Land south of the Mason Dixon, of Gulf waters and Mississippi
tugboat sighs

Land of cane, rice, and watermelon (jungle plums), po' boys, patios,
patois, pecans, pecan pies, pralines, and papier-mâché masks

Place of oak-tree swamps, pine and cypress with hanging gray moss
punctuated by peacocks and pirogues

Land of Creoles, Cajuns, Black Indians, *cawains,* mudbugs, catfish,
and bayou crooners

Region of hot, wet air, heavy with hurricanes, honeysuckle, Irish hash,
and *haints*

Land of Black-faced Zulus, Louis Armstrong, river dragons, and
griots, grits, and gris-gris with loup-garou sunsets

Zone of cockfights, absinthe, *tafia,* anisette, and gospel groups,
congris, and gravel sidewalks

Land of deep-fried fritters, the boot state, trying to keep its head
afloat, the long-lake state, the polluted Ponchartrain, the tooth-
fairy state, the koon-ass state, the red-pepper state, the home of
Tabasco Sauce

The U.S. precinct of Mardi Gras and street parades with great
flambeaux and marching bands, the best in the southland

Home of pelicans and cranes, roaches a finger long that fly and face
you at sunup

Climate of smiling eyes and handshakes and great hugs and southern
how-dos, when every day's a come-on-out-of-the-thundershower
day

Longitude of *lagniappe,* yeah-you-right, and starlit nights

Meridian of *courtbouillon* and hush puppies, gumbo and deathless
days, everyday hallelujahs, crayfish bisque, praying in tongues,
novenas and graveyard gifts of lilies, silver dimes, and *bamboula*

Tropic below sea level, of Scorpio and Saint Joseph salutations, people
who parade, paint faces and forearms like irises and demons

Domain of bayous levees, canals, alligators, Bogalusa, and wrought
iron fences

Neighborhood of Voodoo good luck and yam crops and misbelieves, the password is party, and umbrellas dance

Latitude of leprosy and soybeans, clover and jasmine, mildew, and dead moss

Vicinity of sidewalk cafés and boulevards, preachers and priests with cathedrals of saints' bones and Atchafalaya

Soil of courtyards and river blues, Professor Longhair piano riffs, zydeco, and rosaries on Wednesday nights

The Mahalia Jackson and Fats Domino belt, where the saints come march, where you find your thrill

Terrain of cotton and fireflies, bumblebees, and cats, tiger-striped to Siamese in alleyways and garbage heaps of oyster shells and shrimp leavings (there's more cats per square inch here than most states)

Department of Big Chief, café au lait and beignets, *galait,* and couscous and milk

Sphere of classical and Dixieland jazz, R&B, bayou blues with Baptists, Catholics, and the Ku Klux Klan with jazz singers and souls crying

State of Chocolate City #10 with fortune-tellers and spiritual healers, wall geckos, muddy water, and missionaries

District of sweat and shade, the Second Line, Mississippi moonlit nights, Saturday night suppers in the backyard, the sanctioned speakeasies

Confines of Thibodaux, Tchoupitoulas, Houma, and Louisiana Red in wingtips

Nativeland of jive and jambalaya, the Crescent City—the city care forgot and remembered, "for true."

A Few Words on My Words

This year
I saw my mother's
African eyes in my mirror
My daddy's Creole
face over my skin like a glove.
I answer to two names
smell of coconut and gardenia.

I feed pages
words until they speak
the lives I've seen or heard of
promises made
and promises broken
regularly like hearts or pecans.
I let each line rotate
head to toe
savor each phrase
like a peach cobbler dessert
the cinnamon taste lasts
like a warm smile.

I cut and paste hope
between the lines
keep the pictures
that Black words pour
from my fingertips
stretching like the sun
to paint rainbows in empty spaces.

I Had Forgotten the Loud

—*for Alice Walker*

laughing locusts do at night,
the smell of hot grass
steaming under end-of-summer rain.

    Hurricane Elena was prayed away from New Orleans
by holy women, *haints,* and *loas.*
Hurricanes, the Crescent City crusade,
like bayou music from Allen Toussaint,
the R&B basic brew:
        "Hey there sugar-dumplin'
        let me tell you somethin'…."
from King Floyd or Irma Thomas,
who used to be called colored singers,
or Chitterling Circuit crooners.

    New Orleans leaves a honey taste in my mouth.
The cracked boulevards and weeping willows
shade bare front porches
and call her children home.
I holler, "Hey-now!"
Come southern grown, like
mirliton and magnolias.

Shotgun Life

Shotgun Life I: Home

My chocolate-faced mother
dropped me into my Creole
daddy's hands at home
on the four-poster I
sleep on still.
It was their first new
furniture, bought on account
at Universal, $1.25 a week for
wood posts carved like pineapples
blooming, with a head-
and footboard that
fans out announcing
the AMs of squeezing
between Mother and Daddy,
the crackle of the funnies,
the snorts of his snoring,
and her shhhhhhs,
when only the sparrows and
blue jays outside
sing their morning call,
with brother still dead to
the world, his arms perched
like a runner, while sister
yawns a peek at us
for a coast is clear into
her only privacy, the
first bath of the day
in the claw-foot tub
long enough to stretch inside
a dream or two of
rooms with doors instead
of the shotgun rooms
that run into each other
like all of us all day long, until
cooler evenings on the front porch,

the southerly breezes from
the Gulf, calming
and warming up
spring before
hurricanes come.

Shotgun Life II: Sonnet

    Do you know what it means to miss New Orleans?
Not heat or rain, mosquitoes, flies, but talk,
hey nows between neighbors, mothers, fathers,
sidewalk parties, Claiborne, Back Street Museum parades.
Do you know why natives who left return,
relearn to live cayenne and raise stories
of how they grew under oak trees, willow,
and pine, how streets give way to brollies floating
red bean rhythms that mourn and praise each day
over feathers all plumed with stones and beads?
It means crawfish, *cawain,* mint love, and be
gumbo, as new with no regrets, a dance.

Shotgun Life III: Today

We are a people of this place
where our footprints speak
the *mashuquette* of those
who parade daily before
front porches and side galleries.
The voices of my family
are laughter to my spirit.
The voices of my neighbors
are my days defined
with potato salad across
fences, or crawfish bisque
saved just for me,
my name in all their pots.

West Nile-carrying mosquitoes
run most inside evenings;
here we take turns
braiding hair between thighs
of elder sisters and cousins
or hold jacks contests
or eat fresh boiled crawfish
in season, then wash
the porch with lye
to kill the stains and stench.

The Blessed Mother
still guards back steps,
yards, and porches.
The families inside,
their altars for Lent
glowing in the dusk of misty air.

Sickle-carrying grass cutters
retire into the night.
Angel trumpets open

and fragrance the evening.
Neighborhood dogs, rottweilers
and would-be rottweilers, lie still,
the fullness of a meal sedates
until the wee hours when their
barks will rattle the night
announcing some late-night
passerby or cat on the street.
We give thanks for these days of peace
and pray for quick resolve, the fighting in Iraq.

Shotgun Life IV: Section 8, 2003

Is it a plane, a bomb, 18-wheels crashing?
Hey now, new folks, neighbors, the pumpkin house.
Tell 'em there's a war on! Not here. P-Diddy
Missey, Nellie, OK, I like to jam.
Hip hop, funk up; but this, eardrum piercing,
floorboards erupting, siding rippling, music
now noise, who can feel beats? Think thoughts? Read books?
Folks line sidewalks, barbecue ribs, fresh, hot
crawfish brimming paper platters in heaps,
no one's dancing! Is the music too low?
Must be a birthday bash, maybe a christening,
8 hours, thumping, screeching, no one dancing!

Shotgun Life V: Remembering D

When I was a little person, our house
was everybody's home, cousins with aunts
uncles who kiss as they enter each time.
One aunt lived in the St. Bernard projects,
after her house, li'l bungalow, bought cheap,
the price progress costs poor people, owner
or not. Uncle's wife died, brought me cousin
Dwight, like my brother until 10 years.
Uncle piano-playing-brick-laying man
took D to a new home; our house empty
without D, aunts, cousins, uncles, just a
shotgun, even the grass shed tears AMs.

●

Shotgun Life VI: Roots,
200 Years, Louisiana Purchase

It was 1803, New Orleans, world port,
Mississippi wealth poured steamboats, gamblers,
craftsmen, merchants, bankers, poor, rich, boom growth,
Third largest U.S. city, best land deal
for four cents per acre, American,
but France plus Spain, Latin roots now Creole
when baked African spice spills in Vieux Carrè
Faubourgs, below Canal, downtown music,
shotgun homes, brick walkways, lamb's ear gardens,
semitropics, alligators roam streets.
Mosquitoes wreck composure. Sweat drips.
Ceilings, high heat escapes, shutter sunlight.

Shotgun Life VII: Old School, Circa 1960

Backyard barbecues, oysters on French bread?
Oh yes, family, friends, and folks eat, dance,
count grand, great-grandchildren playing cooncan,
Smokey, Marvin, cold Jax, hot fried chicken,
party under blankets shading the sun,
through dusk, when tipsy aunts, uncles
grinding on dimes in St. Aug grass, shame kids?
Shuck more oysters, fry more catfish, Jack-back
creme sodas, kids napping on loving laps.
Everyone dances now! R&B swoons, wee hours
no birthday bash, no christening, just week's
end, Friday night fish fry, speakeasy on grass.

Red Beans and Ricely Creole Quarters

Nat King Cole Babies
and Black Mona Lisas

Everybody asks: "Really?"
      "Is Mona Lisa your name?"
      "Hey, da Vinci's daughter huh?"
Or, they call another name of note:
      "I'm Mohammed Ali."
Or, you call a friend, leave your name,
and they say:
      "It's some picture calling you!"
Or, they do a double take:
      "Say what?"

See, we are late World War II
boom babies
cuddled, loved, conceived
on backs of pickups,
back porches, and starlit rooms
to Nat King Cole.

The last sister I met named Mona Lisa
came from Chicago in beaded braids;
she was a waitress at the Oakland Athletic Club.
It was Kwanzaa.
She said, "Hey girl" like she knew me.
Said, "Yeah
it was a radio hit, and Nat King Cole
sang it on his own TV show.
In the 1950s, everybody sang 'Mona Lisa.'"

Mona Lisa Wilson and I
went to Xavier Prep a year.
Mona Lisa Carr was a year older,
at Joseph S. Clark—then a trade high—
real cute, a fine cheerleader.
I never knew her, but

I hated her to myself
was ashamed by myself too.

My daddy bears most claim
to calling me.
Mother said I was his baby girl,
and he thought they weren't still able.
Cousin Mildred says
she told him to do it,
said the *Mona Lisa* was on loan
from the Louvre, *all* in the news.

My daddy says in World War II
the day he saw the *Mona Lisa,*
he saw little French boys
catching rats for food in the streets,
and he brought them his G.I. rations
and he thought if he just had another baby girl....

So my sister hated me for so long,
and my brothers didn't pay no mind
about names,
except Junior.
He would sing the "Mona Lisa" song to me
like Uncle Toot
and Uncle Herbert at a piano
and Uncle Clifford
and Mr. Charles.

The late '60s cursed European namesakes.
I reminded many
I was born Black
on a Black block
in the 7th ward

on the back side of New Orleans.
And I always thought
Mona Lisa was Nat King Cole's lover
like "Sweet Lorraine."

    I recalled Iris, Janice, and Joan.
Iris had green eyes, mustard-tanned skin.
        She was littler than me, and we
        always fought for something.
Janice had blue eyes, blond hair, solid blood.
        Her daddy, Mr. John, was handsome, dark tan
        with thick Latin brown hair, and she beat me regularly.

    Joan was jet-black with short, short black hair.
I knew they called her a "tack"
behind her back 'til I come 'round
cause I knew they called my mother that.
Joan thought I was too yellow
and didn't know why I wanted to be
with her, but she was the only one could
outswim, outdance, outdraw, out-make-believe anybody.
They all called me
        a nappy-headed yella nigga
        between scratching and pulling hair:
            Mon' Lisa got nappy hair!
            Mon' Lisa got nappy hair!

    So about the time I stopped frying my hair,
        stopped slapping lye on it,
        or trying tint,
        SunRaa told me
I looked like the *Onni*
or a Zulu queen,
and told me

my hair is sculpture
to crown my nappiness.
And I'll always remember
Nat King Cole singing to me,
loving me like my uncles.

My Creole Daddy I

This is my dad's blue easy chair,
four years old and still too new;
it blues his eyes when he sits
sipping coffee and chicory
more like Mississippi River mud.
This is my dad's green shirt that fades
his eyes gray sometimes when he calls me
by my sister's name now,
but I remember that he wiped my behind
and mopped the floors
when mother tired of walking
all over New Orleans to Congress
Hats for that special applejack brim
he needed to blend with this green shirt
he can no longer button
by himself. I fold family memories with
this green seersucker shirt
thinning finally like Daddy's
snow-white 87-year-old hair.

He walked the beaches of Marsailles,
flew over North Africa,
and whipped up *courtbouillon*
for G.I. buddies like Mr. Neusteder
and Mr. Jackson whenever they landed.
Neusteder called Daddy "nutshot"
he said, since he was a short dude
and would end fights quick with a swift kick;
it never failed. And what was my
mother's name again?

Mr. Jackson brings my daddy
cigarettes Fridays when he visits
his brother Tommy, who sits near my
Daddy's good ear in the day room.

"Jackson brings me menthols
all the damn time; must have
saved his life or something,
ya git me? Ain't seen him in 50
years or more...in *my* company."
"There's no place like New Orleans,
no where yeah!
Cawains used to crawl out the swamp
into my black iron pot."

　　His blue eyes fade under
lids drunk with sleep.
He draws a long swig of near beer.
"O'Doul's tastes just like a Bud!" Daddy affirms.
It satisfies his need for a cold one now.
"You look just like your mother girl,
but you just too *yella*.
Any more bread pudding?"

Daddy's Philosophy II

Daddy loves coffee with chicory
in his cream and sugar
every morning just after 5:30.
Says he eats to keep from
getting hungry.
At 86, he forgets
when and what he eats
especially Häagen-Dazs on a stick,
can inhale one after another with
a smile like sunshine
while peeling away
the plastic wrap.
He sees me watching,
says that's what it means.
"What?" I ask.
"La joie de vivre," he says.
"The joy of life?" I ask.
"Sure, the New Orleans motto," he says,
"the reasons for heavenly hips,
drumstick thighs, and
huggable bellies."
"Yeah, ya right,
even the French say that Daddy."
"No girl, not like we do.
We work like we don't need the money.
We love like we never been hurt.
We dance like nobody's watching.
We eat like there's no tomorrow."

Daddy Poem III: New Orleans Then

Mother says I was born at home
on the four-poster I sleep on still.
Says she dropped me
into Daddy's hands
on a Friday afternoon.
Said I laughed
and laughed again.
Mother says
she didn't even know I was coming
'til she fell down
the back porch steps, a faint spell
or a *haint* visit she thought,
and Daddy thinking
their baby-making days
long since gone.
They were chewing on short grass
in those days Daddy says, so
Mother sewed future dreams
into our dresses and Haspel Brothers
tropical seersucker suits.
Those days, Daddy aimed
to stop working for the cigar factory
to stop passing for white just to keep a job.
He wrapped and shipped the finest tobacco rolls,
he said to feed us. Said, at the cigar factory,
he had to listen to all sorts of
hateful slurs, his stomach churning all day long,
the puke taste rising
to his tongue on the streetcar ride home.
Some days, he walked off his anger,
saved the bus fare for us for soft drinks at dinner,
the five of us on red-beans-and-rice Mondays
with Dixiana French bread,
Tuesdays with cornbread,

Wednesdays with *galait*
(pan-fried shortening bread)
and Barq's creme soda or root beer,
the sweetest days we knew.

Daddy Poem IV

My daddy was a man.
He might have been high yellow but
no one was blacker inside.
That came from his Uncle Henri,
a dark Creole who raised him
after his dad left
his mom and little sister Mildred.
Daddy quit school in the 3rd grade
to work, be the man of the house.
His first job at the cigar factory,
he sorted tobacco, then
rolled watching the wrinkled faces,
happy for a buck a day.
The smell, he said, soaked his skin
and all-weekend washing left traces,
then Mondays rubbed the cigar smell
into his pores again.
I can see him now,
a short, wiry, white-looking Black kid,
who had to keep his mouth shut
so the bosses wouldn't know he was Colored.
With 3rd grade schooling, said he counted
faster than the lot of grown men,
had a knack for organizing,
a way with customers,
never lost a sale, so they
put him on deliveries
where he picked up new customers
all along River Road, driving
around the Pelican State, at 15
bringing home *l'argent* since 8.
My daddy, he was a man.

For Daddy V

    My Daddy
loved three families;
ours was the second.
He outlived two wives,
buried them in a flow of
tears and beer
long as the Mississippi.
Mostly, I remember lots of
hugs and kisses, snuggling
next to Daddy during the
nightly news on TV after
dinner daily, or him
dancing with my dark chocolate Mother
all night at the Autocrat Club
on St. Bernard Avenue.
On Fridays in season, we had crawfish
by the pound, oyster loaves, or
hot sausage sandwiches at Mulés Restaurant
with draft beer we took home in
a stainless steel pot that
sealed like a canning jar.
Springtime brought *cawain,*
and Daddy's expert taking of its head,
then gently removing the neck gland—
a purple thing of poison if burst.
He hung the headless turtle, it still
kicking for three days on the wooden fence,
even its head snapped for hours in the grass.
Never lost a *cawain,* its 21 meat flavors tasting
of beef, pork, fish, and then some.
The turtle eggs, Mother's favorite, promised
youth, health, and sexy eyes, Daddy said.
When he shooed aunts, uncles, and Mother
out of the kitchen, he blended herbs for
sauté and his special roux before stewing.

Big Sunday breakfasts with *galait*—
stove-top shortening bread—and homemade
cocoa, omelets whipped just so, to let Mother sleep late
then wake us for church. He wouldn't come,
just said "pray for me, and I'll get to glory."
Go long so.

On My Block

The milkman sells dream books
and nickel bets once a week.
  Never pay much mind,
  never pay much mind.

Chicken wire fences
keeps out stray cats and kids.
Pecan tree branches hold clotheslines,
wrinkled sheds, and army blankets
that shade the sun from
big galvanized tubs of shrimp,
oysters, and crayfish.
  Never pay much mind.

Louisiana red clay
tracks every living room floor each summer
'til it smokes in red clouds,
when air never cools,
but lights up with fireflies dancing.
  Never pay much mind.

On my block,
the heat sticks to my throat
and steams off the banquette
if you spill a hucklebuck
or a snowball cone.
  Never pay much mind.

Smiling faces from coconut milk
to copper to coffee say,
  "Hey now," or "What'cha know?"
  Never pay much mind.
  Never pay much mind.

Heritage

Shortening-bread mornings with spittoon twangs.
Spilled hot toddies render horseflies suicidal.

Twelve shoe shines and a ninety-minute-john-wait later,
jaywalk to the elementary block with the big kids.

Starched khaki boys and navy-pleated girls
pay draft to patrol kids.
Hip Eddie-Ds and sassy Anna-Maes
swap pint-sized lies in the second grade line.

Peanut butter or cold chicken necks are paper-bagged
because lunch collections are skimmed regularly.
Plantains or banana-fritter desserts
top Jell-O any day.
Handbone down through recess,
and do a signified stroll to the national anthem
all the way back to class.

On hot afternoons of Bible history,
the neighborhood cleaners' man
collects numbers money
and translates dream books.

At three, play cooncan in the streets
and race home on sugarcane stilts before dinner nears.
Catching crayfish by the tail under the house
hightails three mud-blobs in one tub;
the soap never saw white again.

Jambalaya and red wine dinners ease the heat,
privacy needs in a shotgun home, and Mother's prayers,
as the burnt orange sky folds.

Parochial Product

In kindergarten,
I lived black and white.
Before I could count,
I knew who God was.

In first grade,
I constantly prayed for my soul.
The witches wore black and white veils
and prayed the rosary between sentences.

In second grade,
Father took the big girls into the rectory
for catechism.
They came back,
uniforms mussed.
I thought to myself,
praying must be hard work.

In fourth grade,
Sister Grace taught geography, literature,
music,
and that everyone was equal
except us.

In sixth grade,
I almost missed confirmation.
Confessions were weekly;
and by Thanksgiving, I ran out of truths.
By Christmas, I ran out of lies.
By Easter, I had to get new material from
my brother's dirty books,
and Father believed me.

My Cousin My Brother

—for Dwight

When I think of home D,
I remember you and me
playing in the dirt in our backyard on New Orleans Street,
or getting shouted at by Momma (our grandmother)
for doing almost anything related to breathing or walking.

One time that returns to me in dreams and memory
one of many times we played
too close to Momma's roses
and something about Alton
and a beehive. Remember Alton?
Must have been six feet tall,
or so he seemed, and he had big
fat, gentle hands, a middle like
Santa's, and his caramel face
always smiling at us unless
we hurt his feelings or something,
imitating his slurred speech, he
grown and retarded, us too young
and ignorant of life from his eyes.
Anyway, this one time Momma
caught us good, you with a slap
across the head, and me
getting dragged by my nappy
pigtails. Must have been the one
of many times we tried drowning
the yellow jackets' hive in Momma's garden,
but it was her precious rose petals
that fell, and the yellow, prison-striped bees running
Alton into a frenzy. We were happy
and proud of such original fun;
it almost made our whippings worth it.
And while I was convinced we had the
meanest grandmother in the world, it

made us closer as we huddled crying
and angry to be separated from play
and each other for days like a lifetime.

    And now, you a man of music and God,
of family and friends, with time
for hibiscus, jasmine, and me.

French Market Morning

New Orleans tourists have coffee on the river
most mornings.
Beer brewing stench
and shelled oysters
overpower the chicory odor
this butter-shine morning.

The levee is a public park now.
Slaves were sold there.
Once, only Black folks cooked, waited tables,
and swept floors in this café.

Aunt Jemima dolls are made in China now.
White cooks are in the kitchen,
Asian and white waiters at the tables.

The free food line is long and Black.
Black survival wears a different face.
Its pain is older than this market.

French Market Friend

   "Pecans! Pecans!
From de country
by de pound!
What have you Missey?"

   He was an ancient peddler,
seventy-something seven years ago,
sold the freshest everything.

   "Been peddlin' ovva fifty years
me an' me brotha;
a tourist run ovva him
last year."

   His shoulders stooped
from watermelon weight
and time.
Still six feet,
his West Indian coffee color
bronzes in New Orleans' winter sun.
He remembered me every fall he said,
my Catholic school uniform, African-Asian looking eyes,
a few pennies tip with each mango.

   "So, you're a lady now hey?
Pretty little Afro too,
an you nevva fohgot ole Moze de bidda?"

   Moze filled my lunch bag once a week
with free pralines, fresh fruit, and his stories.

   "Hey Missey!
Tell 'em.
Tell 'em you had

coffee wid chicory
at de Café du Monde
wid Mozambique du Cong.
Tell 'em foh me. Tell 'em!"

Recycling Neighborhood Style

Before anybody had more
than five cents for a fat
peppermint candy stick, and
before Nintendo, or HeMan,
or Barbie, Black or white,
before we heard the word "recycle,"
we made our toys
out of Coke tops.
Played double jacks with them.
Used them for lost jacks too.
Nailed them to old anything for decor.

We skated until we dropped,
then outgrown skates
became skateboards or
skate mobiles for block derbies.
We'd nail Coke tops to spell
our names on the mobiles,
or nail them to rotten wooden fences
to make secret codes.
We made miniature floats, with
miniature flags from torn shirts
clipped to wooden clothes pins, waving in
humid heat for miniature Mardi Gras parades
on the banquette.

Clean long-necked Coke bottles
made shapely dolls,
just add mop strings for hair,
and hand sew the latest fashions
out of scraps from castaway clothes.
Clean bottle caps
made now-you-see-it-now-you-don't games,
when the nut was a milk bug,
or an empty peanut shell.

Don't mention Mother's clothesline too loud,
worth gold bouillon.
Cut, it made great twists to set
long wet nappy hair for curls when dried.
Wet, we'd twist and roll that line in our hair
until our arms dropped.
The next day: curls, curls, kinky curls,
good enough to make Shirley Temple cry,
recycling.

    Now, better was clothesline jump rope,
        single or double Dutch,
        eggbeater jump rope,
            with Mother's clothesline.

    Best of all was catching mosquito hawks
by their paper-thin wings.
We'd watch them hover like a helicopter
or a hummingbird.
We'd sit still like a blade of grass
and swoop on the poor mosquito hawk—whoosh it
into a cleaned-out peanut butter jar.
Then, we combed the gravel and oyster shell
streets for cigarette butts, and
fed our prized hawk tobacco.
Ever seen a drunk mosquito hawk?
        Better than a Rambo or Terminator movie.
        Better than Pacman.
Only thing better was a drunk lizard,
or a high praying mantis.
Yes we did.
Got mosquito hawks drunk on cigarette butts,
recycling.

Villanelle for Voodoo

Recall sweet secrets, Gondwanaland love.
Conga divides and blesses the earth and sky.
Women bear birth behind the trail of blood.

A minstrel, late, I sing and die of love.
In red of ram, color of heart that sighs,
recall sweet secrets, Gondwanaland love.

Stench of cinnamon, dance *calinda* love.
Two times joy, one-half sorrow I hide.
Women bare birth behind the trail of blood.
Sun dips blossoms, sky turquoise with doves.
Turn midair; spit past midnight; veil on eyes.
Recall sweet secrets, Gondwanaland love.

Play sword of Solomon, mule-teeth jawbone blood.
burst from flame those burning red-rimmed eyes.
Women bear birth behind the trail of blood.

Nine houses, nine spells, air thick, molasses blood.
Marie LaVeau calls earth's musical sighs.
Recall sweet secrets, Gondwanaland love.
Women bear birth behind the trail of blood.

The Ballad of Marie LaVeau

You must knock three times.
Bring fresh picked flowers
to the grave of Marie LaVeau.
Bright silver candles
penciled crosses
still burn for her Voodoo favors.

Yé Yé Mamzelle Marie,
            Li Konin Tou, la gris-gris.
Yé Yé Mamzelle Marie,
            Li Konin Tou, la gris-gris.

With dusk in sight
women and men
Black and white
dance around a fountain.
Sing Creole songs
all night long,
Marie's eyes on fire.

A long full skirt
curly jet hair,
eyes dark as coals,
a gypsy blouse,
a fish in her mouth,
captivates your soul.

A wave of hands
conjures demons
in the old New Orleans manner.
She blackmailed slaves
of the city's mayor,
deceived officials better.

On Voodoo mornings
Creole secrets spread
as Marie danced Carré Français.
Grapevine songs became evening's call,
for the Marie in the Vieux Carré.

Marriage banns were business plans
in the old New Orleans style.
French gentlemen
kept mulatto girlfriends;
Marie knew each and why.

On the water
hidden by fern,
Maison Blance
her Voodoo haven,
held ancestor rites,
danced like a snake all night,
drank blood from a live kicking chicken.

Marie took a small wax ball,
covered it with feathers,
placed it on a stoop
in pitch-black night
to gather loose hearts and bones.

Marie LaVeau despised
the courts and law,
praying at a Catholic altar,
with three *guiana* peppers,
placed under the judge's seat
freed a man and his son.

Yé Yé Mamzelle Marie,
    Li Konin Tou, la gris-gris.

Yé Yé Mamzelle Marie,
    Li Konin Tou, la gris-gris.

   Congo Square,
strangers beware,
old New Orleans 1830.
Calinda dances
drinking *tafia* from molasses,
Marie was as good as holy.

   Marie LaVeau on Saint Ann's Street,
married Louis Glapion
from Santo Domingo.
Spirit strong
shouting Voodoo calls,
she bore him fifteen children.

   Her daughter
in old New Orleans manner,
kept the secrets of gris-gris alive.
Caramel and cream,
maman and *bébé*,
mixed pots of black-eyed peas
and rice, the divine look
of God into
spell-casting *congris*.

   People believed
three different Maries
were the same identical person.
So Voodoo lived on,
three lifetimes long,
and revived each Saint John's Eve.

In Saint Louis Cemetery Number One
a white headstone reads:
        Marie Philome Glapion.

    You must knock three times.
Bring fresh picked flowers
to the grave of Marie LaVeau.
Bright silver candles
penciled crosses
still burn for her Voodoo favors.

Yé Yé Mamzelle Marie,
        Li Konin Tou, la gris-gris.
Yé Yé Mamzelle Marie,
        Li Konin Tou, la gris-gris.

The Last Mile

It comes like a rider on a horse.
You hear it long before it arrives,
the empty silence broken
like a clap of thunder in a scared
heart too beaten to break.
You smell it too,
the rot coming in slowly,
the way gnats and moths wander
toward light.
If you're lucky, it's
announced, devil's bread growing
in a yard,
still an unwelcome visitor.
Digging it up melts the fungus, but
death keeps coming like termites
and lice in an old shed.
So, within the city of the living,
we prepare for
the city of the dead,
the quiet place of narrow,
St. Augustine grass-lined walkways,
of cement-covered brick,
or marble and granite slab
tombs stacked like little houses
above the ground,
listing families and friends long gone.

First, take off the shoes, and
no new shoes at the service
or cemetery, or the
dead will rise, jealous,
to get them and you.

Second, cover the mirrors,
so the soul can't stay here.

Next, unplug clocks, stop time,
and face the dead east to meet God
in glory, and the here will
be gone after now.

Then a wake, a last visit with
the shell, the effigy of the
one gone, last respects for the living
who loved and love on.
It may be for an evening
or a week, a chance to pray
and wish the soul well on
its way, its new
life after living.
Now, the living bakes and cooks
for kin, so they may grieve and
suspend caring for three days.
The First Line.

Pray, grieve and cry and ache
and holler and faint from loss
and emptiness, for the spaces once
filled no more, for the
times together, alive in memory only,
so the living may go on again
until the next time.

In the city of the dead,
where the cleaned whitewashed
tombs are flooded with flowers,
mums mostly and carnations of
every hue, a lily or two
among wrought-iron fences
or in vases on the small shelves.
Here, the rich and the famous

bear epitaphs:

FAMILLE VVE. PARIS	FAMILY WID. PARIS
née LAVEAU	born LAVEAU
Ci-Git	Here lies
MARIE PHILOME GAPION	MARIE PHILOME GLAPION
décédée le 11 Juin 1897	deceased June 11, 1897
agée de soixante-dewx ans	sixty-two years old
Elle fut bonne mère,	She was a good mother,
bonne amie et	a good friend and
regrettée par tous	missed by all
ceux qui l'ont connue.	who knew her.
Passants priez pour elle.	Passersby, please pray for her.

St. Louis Cemetery No. 1

In the city of the dead
you can visit, kneel the stations
of the cross at St. Rock cemetery.
Make a novena, and
pray a petition with lit candles
for favors, or pilgrimage on
Good Friday when you can pray
and leave money at each of nine
churches, and a husband is promised
before the year ends. For luck
pick a four-leafed clover, the red ones
from the blood of a
bride-to-be, whose suicide
marks her lover's grave here.

The last release is the best.
The Second Line dance.

Dance, swoon, and ride your grief
like there's no tomorrow.
The melodies will sway like
waves in a hurricane, hurried,
smashing, then softly calm
before the last rush of grief.

There is a sadness
in the silence after death.

Then grieve and cry and ache
and holler and faint from loss
and emptiness, for the spaces once
filled no more, for the times together, alive in memory only,
so the living may go on again
until the next time.

A Taste of New Orleans in Haiku

i
Mardi Gras Indians
red beans and rice, hot sausage
dancing Second Lines

ii
Allelu Sundays
giving thanks, blessings, family
panné meat dinners

iii: Heard on the Street
After 9-11
white people like niggas yeah
suddenly, we, US

iv
On Mardi Gras Day
skeletons remind all folks
you might be next yeah

v
Going to the Mardi Gras
li'l kids, old kids, everyone
celebrates the day

vi
Red beans and rice day
washing clothes all day Monday
add French bread, salad

vii
Butter beans Wednesdays
Barq's root beer a midweek treat
everyone's home

viii
All Catholic girls
dream themselves as nuns some day
dreams echo a lifetime

ix
After Mardi Gras
winter ends and spring begins
Lent, azalea blooms

x
Before the A/C
window fans, lemonade, sweat
breeze, oak tree shade, smiles

xi
Summers with A/C
now, no one sleeps on the porch
safe behind iron doors

xii
Jazz Fest, who would think
April, May, good as Mardi Gras
almost summertime

xiii: Haiku for Daddy
His African heart
his Creole blue eyes, light skin
his core, New Orleans

Summer in New Orleans

        Such sweet thunder
with sidewalks that talk of
generations of families
from music makers—
those clapping gospel riffs
and alleluia Sundays in neighborhood churches—
to food fed spirits
when *cawain* is a spring event
of 21 meat tastes stewed or
red beans and rice raise the Monday
blues to rhapsody
for every feuding face that
genuflects before grottoes,
of the Blessed Virgin,
the mini altars between
many shotgun steps,
the Blessed Mother,
the sweetest protector
of Catholic schoolgirl dreams
and prayers of the faithful.
New Orleans of sunshine
and novenas, prayers of petition
and thanks for favors
granted through Crescent City
Saints: St. Jude, St. Peter Claver, Sts. Martin and Anthony,
St. Raymond, St. Raphael, St. Maria Garetti....
The kneeling down and incense-prayers going up
for loved ones and friends in need.
Blessings of St. Augustine grass,
greening faubourgs, tall spread oaks and
Louisiana pines, rain for
Camellia blooms even in winter,
and in summers of heat and showers
like a million mosquito hawks tap dancing on roof tops,
such sweet thunder.

On Writing

I knock on white space to speak,
pour Black ink like blood
to mark meaning on a blank page.
The page, pregnant with thoughts,
bares words and more words
each line like night jasmine,
Gardenia, or skunk
spread as magnolia leaves
windblown in early fall.
Ideas take flight,
whirl with hurricane force
or fall flat, silent like
the eye of a hurricane,
a false end to fury
where words return
whipping meaning drunk
with images flowering,
like the Chinese 100-day blossoming pink tree,
Dr. Fujita's Japanese monkey-sliding smooth trunk,
outside of his window in Gentilly Gardens,
what we call crepe myrtle
with fat-bellied
brown-gray sparrows,
singing again.

Black Creole Love

This Afternoon…

We seeped like light
through a closed door's crevices
disregarding chain and lock.
Both having recent lessons,
we swapped precautionary measures,
traded safety hints,
and proceeded to open ourselves raw,
enjoying fresh subjects,
verbs,
and tender
easy loving.

Email: Hey Now

i.

Thanks for your call,
your voice on the line, a welcome.
I remember when I first saw you
        towering over the Whole Foods cashier.
I forgot that strangers remain so until the first Hi
        opens one moment like a new letter in the mail.
It hurt me that I was too chicken to talk,
        busied myself among apples, grapes, and blueberries
        spread like corn on the ground for pecking,
because I believed walking up to your proud blackness
        that filled the place like a Zulu king or a Denzel
        needed more than the shyness I held in these palms.
What I really wanted was to smile, hold your hand,
        and follow you anywhere.
I thought I needed to be high-heeled and business-bank suited
        to catch your eye,
but your voice smiling at me on the phone tonight,
the sound of maybe....

ii.

I want to speak your language
hold your words in my heart
a shed from a storm.
I want to wear your spirit,
that glad sunlight you share daily,
a beacon of safety at sea.
Here is my ear to drink your cares,
my eyes to watch you blossom.
Here is my hand; hi to you.

Distant Lover Poem

i.

The night we...
tears fell
I was so happy.
Slept so hard,
I snored in waves
that woke me
feeling in balance
breathing in step
with our heartbeats.

The kitty-cat purred with us
and watched.

ii.

It's a good thing
you don't live here
'cause I might want to park
permanently in the hollow
under your arm
and next to your chest
the spot made just for me
snuggled in the crest of your neck
where I belong.

iii.

Sweetheart,
in the evening
your voice on the phone
hugs my heart
holds it up
for a kiss
and caresses
me for the night.

When We...

When I need you to hold me, and
you lean just inches away, maybe
I can't tell you how I need to, sometimes,
sounds easy that one can just say something
to someone, but some words come like bricks in
your throat, and the brow bleeds, and female parts
butterfly, and I surrender to your need for
a hug in your eyes when you can't tell
me, but I can hear it in your purr some-
times, in your pouring over me like honey,
hot and golden, touching inch by inch,
finger to fold in heat, and the way those
chestnut eyes follow me like an airplane
when we need to be held, and we can't say.

The First 30 Days

    It took one day
to hear your heart
two days to sense your spirit.

    It took one week
to cough up your fear
two weeks to calm your anger
three weeks to ignite your love.

    It took one month
to know the gentle in your touch
            the raw in your words
            the love in your voice.

    It took one hour to hear your call
two hours to raise your fury
four hours to cultivate the bitter
five hours to land at a wall
eight hours to say I'm sorry
ten hours to forgive
twelve hours to make up
with a lifetime to go.

Charm Fails Death

I should seek wisdom
befriend courage, sense, and insight.
I tried to repair
an old garment with new cloth.
Death is no one's fool twice.
I have learned
all flowers of a tree
don't grow fruit,
and dross may sparkle like gold,
and I loved too quick,
so there was no love,
and I lived too quick,
so there was no life,
and repentance cures no regret,
but wrings a heart worse than torture,
and these tears of blood
echo loss forever.

Deuces Running Wild

I share rooms with another lady.
We swap scars like a card game
accumulating spreads
of like disappointments
that help us approach the deck carefully.
We ponder each trump in hesitation
knowing what is on the table.
We check the kitty frequently
realizing
only time can teach us
when to hold,
when to bid,
when to fold.

Telling Poem

I'm not afraid to look
and like what I see in a man.

I'm eager to enjoy and be and learn
what I can from a man.

I'm slow to trust, to understand
the distance between
myself and a man.

I don't know
how long it takes to grow
to learn to open
the gates of love
for a man.

I do know
how to take a minute
to hours and days to
months and years listening
to learn who a man is.

I'm naive enough
and kind enough
and gentle enough
and interesting enough
to offer friendship
to a man.

I'm smart enough
have lived enough
and learned enough to wait
for a real exchange
with a man.

I'm ambitious enough
and strong enough
and giving enough
to want the best from
a man and get it.

I'm patient enough
and caring enough
and open enough
to share with a man
and mean it.

I'm sensible enough,
affectionate enough,
and sincere enough
to care deeply
for a man.

I know enough
to lift the curtains,
unveil my heart,
and accept
caring from a man.

I've studied enough
and learned enough
and seen enough to know
that love is possible.

I'm content enough
and happy enough
and fulfilled enough
to try again.

Like Langston Hughes Did

I am living
to heal the hole
in my heart
from Middle Passage
saltwater burns
to kiss the earth
of my mother/fatherland
to become one
with my ancestors
the Ashanti, Ibo, Housa, Yoruba,
Pygmy, Dogun, Wallof, Fulani,
Zulu, Watusi, Mandingo, Nubian
my brothers
my sisters
my mother's great-great-grandmothers
my father's great-great-grandfathers
my ancient homeland
my people with ages and ancient temples in their eyes
saltwater Africans
returned to me
the salt burning my eyes,
a cleansing of heart.

Red Beans and
Ricely Black

Song for Elder Sisters

    Those surviving sisters
born to farms
over the tracks
or backs of towns,
the southern poverty belt,
coming up chopping cotton, planting potatoes.
        "She went to the river
        couldn't get across.
        She paid three dollars
        for an old blind horse.
        One leg broke,
        the other leg cracked.
        Good God y'all
        how those crackers cracked."
They whacked all morning, yakked all night.
Still sister kept on her way
with a hope and a prayer.

School ended at ten,
and hard knocks took hold,
on poverty's edge, her song,
the cheapest amusement.
So, singing sung dawn to dusk
like hers before her
in slave yards or sopping floors.
        "She went down the road,
        the road was muddy,
        stubbed her toe,
        made it bloody.
        Sung her song,
        hard and long."

In shotgun homes,
on front porches,

hair tied back or braided with the dust of years,
she stands guard for bloodlines
as solemn and fruitful as pecan trees.

Mother with Me on Canal Street, New Orleans

My mother's face
in the sepia photo
like an Egyptian mural,
a painting speaking my past.

My mother was so chocolate
so sweetly smiling
full of hugs and
how're ya doings that
when my yella face
hit the front of the St.
Charles Avenue street car,
riding on Canal Street,
and she let me sit on
the only seat, the Ponds-smelling
gray-haired lady asked us,
"You keeping her for a white family uptown?"
Well, my mother's face broke
into a belly laugh and so did mine
and she told that lady,
"Oh no, we live downtown,
and like it just fine."
Then when we stepped on to
the steamy pavement
and the bus pulled off,
my mother hugged me
tight and told me that
I might be yella but I was
Black as her, and I could
hold my head up forevva
cause my heart was pure
and Black just like hers; and
chocolate was good
and meant to be savored

whether it was light or dark
and don't evva forget it; so, I
said no indeed mother, but
I sure wished my chocolate
showed brown like hers
and white folks wouldn't have
to ask me if I was a war
baby or a Chinee or anything
other than what I was,
so happy to be just
my little Black self;
and when we get home,
I'm gonna make her Papa tell me
about how when folks be
carrying shit in their pockets,
it makes 'em stink. Alright,
she said, don't get uppity now;
let it go then. So we
went home holding
hands all the way.

For My Brothers

They come from Kingston or Lagos
Carolina or Chicago
in second-generation struts
from Jackson or Detroit
New Orleans and Oakland
tipping a dip in their walks
leaning under Stetsons
solid Black in three-piece suits
echoing yellow to black in T-shirts
against muscles earned on American streets
like moles with big lips
and ebony eyes of almonds or diamonds raw;
some too broken to bitch,
others speak in labors and art,
fight, push-the-word execs.
Some grow their hair in dreads or
knots crying
        "Yeah, that's me.
        I don't fit. You won't let me fit anyways."
Yet they live to rejoice life,
sing the blues, jazz the magic they know,
each move a mojo,
warm and fresh like new grass.
They come carrying cures of love.
It is all many have
like a sunset and a song
and being a man
a Black man
conjuring a day at a time
with honey smiles and chocolate touches.
They speak proverbs in pungent tongues
of Friday night juju
from pyramids and one-room flats.
They taste of good luck
fill you like Voodoo

healing the deep scars or busting them open.
They whisper spit from banjo bellies,
smell like other worlds.
Keep on, bloom
sun-soaked Sweet Willies.

jim crow

jim crow was the unofficial stamp of segregation,
the label, the law,
a people pigeonholed
to lesser status, the Negro problem,
imperialism with a capital in WA, D.C.
colonialism with a capital U.S.
second-class citizens, with no justice, no opportunities,
ghettoes formed by force of law.
Colored was a flag for bad news,
No Negro officers
No Negro welders
No Negro plumbers
No Negro electricians
No Negro truck drivers
Negro meant NO!
No Negroes in hospitals or hotels or soda fountains.
We were pushed aside
out of side doors and into back doors
into poor schools and worse housing
and no share of the America we built with our backs
and sweat and tears.
We were born in Colored homes, taught in Colored schools,
went to Colored churches, Colored YMCAs, and Colored YWCAs
Colored balconies at the movies
Colored-only water fountains
Colored-only side windows at the groceries.
So, we made soul food, hucklebucks,
corn pone, and bread pudding,
gumbo, and *greyas*.
We made gospel, rhythm and blues, jazz.
They told us we had "equal but not
identical accommodations."
We were separate and unequal
like espresso and whipped cream
restricted, confined, relegated, then blended by gravity and grace.

So, we made juke joints, fish fries and
suppers (*our* speakeasies) in the backyard.
And with our uncommon common sense,
it took us some forty years to find
we did all right together.

End Notes

    Southerners sip
café au lait with *galait*
pan-fried and flat
like the raindrops this
morning. We smell the
rain before it comes
to visit, the damp
aroma its calling
card.

    All legs, feet,
and "hey nows," the sun
kissed us olive from
New World Louisiana Creole gumbo,
like the *greyas*
of whatever's in the kitchen
sink, with
mirliton, parsley,
and onion to taste.
No one yells
cause we carry
"how're ya doing's" and
"s'il vous plaits" between *"pas connais."*
We save our clothes,
make groceries,
wash and scrub the porch and
the banquette with lye
after hucklebuck spills
or boiled crawfish leavings
to clean and erase evil spells.
No insults shake us. Naivete warms us.
Our hands toughen after
sewing machine needles tattoo
lives of customs and costumes each Mardi Gras.
We outlaugh enemies,

close louvers to their curses, retreat to the gallery
where lemonade and laughter lives.

I ready my kerchief and
umbrella for the next
Second Line and catch new tales.

The N Word

—for Carolyn M. Rodgers

We all say it,
but we're not supposed to anymore.
There's the daily,
"Who'd you call a nigger?" Or,
"Only niggers talk like that!"

They tell me,
I shouldn't use the N word in the new millennium,
in my poems, in hushed raps to a lover in the dark,
or in any talk I might give.

They say the N word is a holdback
to jim crow times they'd rather
forget, so not mentioning it
eases the N word from memory.
Besides, it's disrespectful, vile, like the doo-doo of our history.
And, we've come up to hyphenated status with
origin of great pharaohs and queens,
that the N word is no
longer relevant to our tomorrows.

So I say that I only call a nigger
a nigger when appropriate,
such as in the case of dumb niggers, mean niggers,
lucky niggers, big-leg niggers, and big-butt niggers,
fat niggers, big-lipped, and no-lipped niggers,
kinky-hair niggers, and good-hair niggers,
kiss-ass niggers, and kick-your-ass niggers,
controversial niggers, famous niggers,
has-been niggers, movie-star niggers,
ball-playing, beer-drinking, coke-sniffing niggers,
skinny, dread-locked niggers, and vegetarian niggers,
grease-monkey niggers, and
cowboy niggers on horses in Texas and Oakland, California,

northern niggers who think they ain't niggers,
beatnik niggers, hippy niggers,
blues-singing, jazz-bopping niggers, and
rhythm-and-blues swinging niggers, and
hip-hop, baggy-butt-pants niggers,
and we all know at least two sorry-assed niggers—
niggers with a handful of gimme
and a mouthful of much obliged—
important niggers and niggers who think they're important,
ugly niggers that'll make a jailbird run free,
pretty niggas that'll make the sun sit on a tree,
old, corny, jive niggers with their:

> "What's the word?"
> "Thunderbird!"
> "What's the price?"
> "Thirty twice!"

There's neo-jive, monosyllabic niggers with their "Word!"
Wise niggers like Oneida—a die-hard nationalist nigger—
who says:

> "Niggers and flies
> I do despise.
> The more I see niggers,
> the more I like flies."

Canceling the *N* word is like throwing out the baby
when her clothes don't fit.
We're not speaking of nice Colored men, but
trifling niggers without a pot to piss in,
no-'count, nosey niggers—
who mind your business and mine—
brick-head red niggers, and jungle-fever niggers.
This ain't no

> eeney-meeney-miney-mo flack.

This is niggerness and
nigger raps for doctor niggers
and teacher niggers and

good niggers.
You know,
if they've got you've got niggers.
Real, down-to-the-ground,
slap-it-on-your-thighs-and-laugh niggers,
bones-playing niggers,
street-smart niggers,
and mysterious-come-alive-after-five niggers,
those midnight-rambler, all-night gambler niggers,
sweet niggers, and naturally blue-black, brown, yellow niggers,
and uppity niggers.

    I've got a neighbor,
a bona fide, high-yellow tenth generation
Creole nigger.
Says she's
not Black, or a Negro.
She is Colored.
That's what it says on
her birth certificate.
My Colored neighbor hates sorry-assed,
incompetent niggers.
Says she "don't want nothin' to do
with anything Black."
She won't call a
nigger plumber,
no nigger electrician,
no nigger carpenter, 'cept family.
Only thing a nigger can do for her
is get out of her way or die.
But worse she says are Oreo niggers,
lukewarm niggers, and
bourgeoisie niggers with their
Gucci, Pucci, Nike Air Pump, BMW
or Merced niggers.

You can bleach your skin.
You can texturize your hair.
You can eat crawfish with a fork,
but you're still a nigger, my nigger.

You're *my* nigger, if you don't get no bigger.
And, if you *do* get bigger, you'll be
my bigger nigger!

"Where y'at my nigger?
You're my main nigger,
my favorite turd,
and that ain't no shit!"
Hey my nigger.
You know, you're my nigger—
my nerve, my jelly preserve.

And for folks who talk about
people like me,
people my color (yellow),
they say
I don't know my identity
by the biological thinness of melanin.
First of all,
all niggers only been a nigger
a few times in their lives,
and I'm happy to say that
I'll only be a nigger
six times in my life:
a nigger baby
a nigger girl
a nigger woman.
Though I was a crippled nigger,
and I am a good nigger,
but one day I'll be a dead nigger.

So, I hope that no card-carrying
African American, or no stamped, certified,
Colored, or Negro is ever insulted
cause I call a nigger *my nigger.*

Nigger please!

We've Come This Far

It isn't hard to see
how Africans in America embraced
a western church.
God was no stranger.
God woke up the day,
   cried over anger,
   calmed the nights with starlight,
     and gave Africans in America serenity as a shield.

We suckled pink babies,
   didn't kill them.
We turned cheeks,
   lowered our heads,
but our hearts rose in spirit,
   volcanoes of culture.

I've walked among the hundreds of faces
   humbled in the presence of peace.
I've witnessed the meek, the thousand smiles of grace.

Because God called,
Negroes answered as Christian soldiers.
Blacks took to Jesus like a crawfish to mud.
God is no stranger in our homes.
We are soldiers at war under divine charge,
prayer the only down payment,
   faith the daily deposit.

Whatever the cost of time
God paid in death to jim crow, integration,
   rights, civil rights,
   affirmative selves furnished each generation,
   at least for those about the Lord's business.
The constant cost, a listening heart,
   to the Greatest Voice to echo.

So we rap to the Lord regularly,
        consult on corners at church,
        and in the quiet of a look.

We've come this far by faith.

Glossary

bamboula: traditional African dances that slaves performed in Congo Square and at Voodoo celebrations on Lake Ponchartrain. Some participants went into trances. These dances were outlawed during slavery, but were practiced in secret.

bébé: [Creole from the French] baby, a term of endearment, often shortened to *bey*

Black-Faced Zulus: masked members of the Zulu Social and Pleasure Club as they appear on Mardi Gras Day

Black Indians (Mardi Gras Indians): Black men from New Orleans neighborhoods who mask as Indians in elaborate costumes of ostrich plumes and beaded designs. A typical suit takes one year to produce. Each "tribe's" Big Chief adopts a color and parades on Mardi Gras Day, or St. Joseph's Day, referred to as Super Sunday.

Blood: of African blood, a Black person

Bogalusa: a city in Louisiana

calinda dances: orgy-like Voodoo dances performed by slaves on Sundays in Congo Square through the mid-nineteenth century

Carré Français: [French] "French square," another name for the Vieux Carré in New Orleans.

cawain: swamp turtle, said to have 21 meat tastes.

Chitterling Circuit (Chitlin Circuit): the round of tours Black musicians made through the south and north in "Colored Only" nightclubs during Jim Crow days.

Congo Square: seeking to curb the influence of West Indian immigrants in the early 1800s, the New Orleans city council prohibited assemblies of slaves for dancing and other purposes except on Sundays in an open place. Congo Square, an open field northwest of the city limits, became the place for slave dances. In the later nineteenth century, it was the site of the old parish prison; now it is the home of Armstrong Park.

congris: dish of black-eyed peas and rice cooked with sugar, used for casting spells. Also, a good-luck dish served with cabbage in many Black homes at the New Year; represents the eyes of God watching over a household.

courtbouillon: stewed fish, usually redfish or sheephead, prepared with highly seasoned gravy.

Crescent City: nickname for New Orleans, so named because the city curves around the Mississippi.

dream books: a book that interprets dream images and assigns the image a number, which carries considerable luck according to most Black people.

Those "dream" numbers influence bets on horse racing or lotteries.

flambeaux: flame carriers accompanying floats at Mardi Gras parades.

Frank Fitch: the poet's maternal grandfather; a bricklayer and Baptist minister.

galait: [Creole] shortening bread; a pan-fried bread of basic dough with no yeast.

Grand Marshall: the leader of the Second Line dance in a funeral procession or parade.

greya: [Creole] tomato gravy added to any protein or meat.

griot: [French] a storyteller who passes on the history of the people

gris gris: Voodoo fetish, charm, amulet, or talisman of power for good luck, also used to cast spells, thought to be of African origin.

guiana peppers: peppers used in casting spells.

haint: [Creole] patois for ghosts or spirits of the dead.

handbone: Rhythmic hand-clapping with thigh and chest slapping that accompanies song or tales, and brought by Africans to the New World. It imitates drumbeats and is a popular past time activity since slavery.

"Hey there, Sugar Dumpling....": from a popular New Orleans rhythm and blues song, "Groove Me," written and performed by King Floyd

high-yellow nigger: in the South, a very fair-skinned Black (with little or no visible African features) who can pass for white; in the North, any fair-skinned Black with an olive skin tone.

Houma: "red" in language of Native American tribe of the same name living in Louisiana; currently the largest tribe in the state. Also the name of a city in Louisiana.

hucklebuck: originally, colored water sweetened with corn or cane syrup served in a paper cup; now, frozen fruit juice, Kool-aid, or other sweetened beverage in a paper cup (also called "Dixie cups" or "frozen cups"); sometimes fruit is added.

Irma Thomas: "The Soul Queen of New Orleans;" popular singer and performer of rhythm and blues.

jusqu'aux bontemps rouler: [Creole from French] "let the good times roll," New Orleans city motto.

lagniappe: [Creole from Old French] "something extra;" a continuation of an age-old West-African tradition of giving a purchaser a little extra to encourage repeat business.

Loa: Voodoo god personality that possesses a child or believer while the participant is in a trance. Believers trance to communicate to spirits; in turn, spirits speak or act through the entranced believer, during which time the believer may change physical characteristics, mannerisms, and speech, and become the spirit for the period of the trance.

loup-garou: famous New Orleans *haint* or spirit with a wolf head and large black bird wings; said to haunt the garrets and rooftops in the French

Quarter as well as swamps.

Maison Blanche: [Creole from French] "white house," name for the long-term residence of Marie Laveau.

Major Lance: popular rhythm and blues performer.

Mardi Gras: [French] "Fat Tuesday" (Shrove Tuesday); the last day of the carnival season; affectionately called *Mardi Gras Day.*

Marie Philome Glapion: the family name of Marie Laveau; the name on her tombstone.

mashuquette: [Creole] "gossip"

mirliton (meliton): a favorite native vegetable in the eggplant family, called "cayote pears" in the West.

mulatto: [Creole from French] first generation offspring of a Black and a white person; also a person of mixed Black and white ancestry.

onni: ancient Nigerian head sculpture in bronze.

panné: breaded veal cutlets, a popular Creole dish

pas connais: [Creole from Old French] "don't know"

Saint John's Eve: June 23; the largest and most important Voodoo celebration of the year, when practitioners visit graves and make offerings of money and flowers. It is said that dead Voodoos converse with those praying on St. John's Eve through tomb walls.

Second Line: a walk or step dance; the joyful walk on the return from a burial (the loved one's troubles of this life are over, mourning turns to great rejoicing for the living), the First Line is the sad walk to the grave.

shotgun: a long, narrow house (single or double) in which the rooms are in a direct line front to back; ideally, one can look through the front door and see out the back door; a common style for slave homes. Actually, some shotguns are not straight through, but all are considered historic. Historians have connected this style to the architecture of the Caribbean and West Africa.

suppers: neighborhood speakeasies; generally held on Friday or Saturday nights, families might serve plates of food (chicken or fish with potato salad and pastry) to raise money or to socialize. Tables would be decorated with candles and wildflowers, and people could purchase drinks.

tack: Derogatory name for a Black person with hair that supposedly doesn't grow or is very short.

tafia: Dark, thickly sweet alcoholic drink distilled from molasses and used in Voodoo.

Tchoupitoulas: "people by the river or water." Purportedly a Native American Indian tribe honored by a street name and related to the Houma Indians.

Vieux Carré: [Creole from the French] "old square;" another name for the French Quarters, the original walled city of New Orleans bordered by

Canal Street, North Rampart Street, Esplanade Avenue, and the Mississippi River. Later it became the trade center of New Orleans.

Voodoo: African religion of the Yoruba from Dahomey and Benin, brought to the New World and practiced in the Caribbean as well as New Orleans.

Yé Yé Mamzelle Marie, Li Konin tou La Gris Gris: [Creole] "Spirit gives you the power of healing and magic; the power of the Spirit is yours."

yella: yellow; fair-skinned Black, can be used in a derogatory or affectionate manner.

About the Author

Mona Lisa Saloy is associate professor of English and director of creative writing at Dillard University. She received her PhD in English and MFA in creative writing from Louisiana State University and her MA in creative writing and English from San Francisco State University.

Displaced by Hurricane Katrina, Saloy is a visiting associate professor of English and creative writing at the University of Washington for the 2005/2006 academic year.